LOOKING INTO
THE EYE OF GRIEF

Also by Marlene Enderlein

Retirement: Death of a Career

LOOKING INTO THE EYE OF GRIEF

An Illustrative View of the Essence of Grief

Marlene A. Enderlein

FRANTHIS PUBLISHING
San Francisco

Published by Eranthis Publishing
San Francisco, California

Copyright 2024 by Marlene A. Enderlein

First published 2024

Printed in the United States of America on
acid-free paper

ISBN-13: 979-8-218-32883-2 (pbk)
ISBN-13: 979-8-218-32884-9 (ebk)

Library of Congress Control Number:
2023922319

In loving memory of my parents,
brother, and husband,
for their deaths caused me to look
into the eye of grief

No one ever told me that grief felt so like fear.

—C. S. Lewis, *A Grief Observed,* 1961

CONTENTS

Contents

INTRODUCTION

Grief. How does one even begin to define this enigma? Suffering the loss of a loved one or something cherished not only causes emotional anguish but also affects one physically, cognitively, socially, culturally, behaviorally, spiritually, and philosophically; grief's expanse and depth affect one's entire mind, body, and spirit. Dictionaries provide succinct parameters describing grief as significant emotional distress or sorrow related to the loss of a loved one, but this is a mere shadow of the true essence of grief, which extends beyond such narrow boundaries. Only when an individual assigns their own personal feelings and experiences to grief will they truly recognize its enormity.

Every person on earth will experience loss during their lifetime, yet, though loss is universal, each person's loss will be unique. Many factors will influence their reactions and responses to grief.

The circumstances of a loved one's death can have a major impact on the grieving pattern of a surviving loved one. If the death was anticipated and peaceful, loved ones were afforded time to say their goodbyes. Although anticipatory grief does not prepare a person for the immense loss they feel upon the death of a loved one, they are able to prepare for the impending death. In contrast, a sudden, unexpected death due to an accident, suicide, homicide, drug overdose, or acute medical event makes grieving more difficult, as loved ones had no time to prepare for the loss, and they may have feelings of guilt or significant anger toward those responsible for the loved one's death. In cases of drowning, kidnapping, or plane crashes, where a loved one is missing, ambiguous loss is most traumatic and devastating, as the surviving loved ones are left with no answer for or resolution to their loss.

An individual's cultural background can affect how they process grief. One's culture is based on traditions, customs, beliefs, and values. The death of a loved one is a shared and social event that affects many others, as it creates a void not only in the lives of surviving loved ones but also in the family structure and in the community to which the person belonged. Cultural rituals provide ways to express grief, in addition to providing community, comfort, and support. Some cultures encourage wailing as a sign of respect, whereas in other cultures, the outward demonstration of grief is thought to interrupt the spirit's journey into the next world. There are gender differences in some cultures, dictating that women may grieve but men are expected to be stoic. Cultural mores can be helpful following a death when there is chaos and loss of structure; however, at times, adherence to cultural traditions and behaviors may not align with one's beliefs or the deceased's wishes, creating conflict or difficulties within the family unit or even complicating the individual's grief journey.

The person who died and their relationship to surviving loved ones can also influence one's emotional response to grief and the ability to cope with the loss and integrate it into one's life. The death of an infant, child, or adult child can be particularly difficult, as it opposes the expected laws of nature. Furthermore, how dependent the surviving loved one was on the deceased can be an important factor in how they process and cope with the loss. Some losses may be disenfranchised, such as the loss of a stillborn infant, a loss due to miscarriage, a loss secondary to suicide, or the loss of a companion pet. Disenfranchised losses are difficult to mourn, as they are often not recognized by society, leaving the bereaved to grieve alone, with no means of support.

How one regards the meaning of death also will affect how one processes the loss. We are a death-denying and death-defying nation. The word *death* is rarely uttered, but more than two hundred euphemisms are used for death, such as "at peace," "passed away," or "no longer with us." Death is something to fear and a battle against which to rage, a battle to lose only at the end. Those who fear death will have a more difficult time processing their grief. However, those who perceive that death is an inherent part of life will find it less difficult to achieve meaning and purpose in life following their loss. Swiss American psychiatrist Elisabeth Kübler-Ross (1975) stated,

> It *is* hard to die, and it will always be so, even when we have learned to accept death as an integral part of life, because dying means giving up life on

this earth. But if we can learn to view death from a different perspective, to reintroduce it into our lives so that it comes not as a dreaded stranger, but as an expected companion to our life, then we can also learn to live our lives with meaning—with full appreciation of our finiteness, of the limits on our time here. (p. 6)

Psychological studies have shown that the personality of the bereaved can also direct the trajectory of their grief journey. Critical thinkers who view things logically tend to avoid the emotional side of loss. Those who are insightful and creative are more expressive and open to their feelings of loss. Outgoing and practical individuals value their relationships and will frequently hide their feelings to protect others from the difficulties they are carrying. Then there are the problem solvers, who possess the necessary coping mechanisms and are well equipped to shoulder the burden resulting from their loss.

The preceding factors can contribute to a unique grief experience and color the expression of the feelings of grief.

EXPRESSIVE ART HISTORY

Archaeologists have found that works of art and the use of symbolic expression were created by Neanderthals prior to the arrival of *Homo sapiens* more than fifty thousand years ago. Primitive cave art has provided a glimpse into the ancient world. Over time, these artistic expressions and symbols became means of communication, before writing was invented.

In the early 1900s, noted Swiss psychiatrist Carl Jung developed an analytic theory that recognized that the human brain is composed of both a conscious and an unconscious. Whereas consciousness includes one's emotions, feelings, and values, the unconscious contains unrealized wishes, needs, thoughts, and ideas. Jung's theory of analytical psychology recognized the mind–body–spirit connection by linking the person's conscious and unconscious. Jung is considered the father of art therapy, as he discovered that drawing and art were means to gain access to the unconscious mind and ultimately offer insight into a person's emotions. He wrote,

> Often it is necessary to clarify a vague content by giving it a visible form. This can be done by drawing,

painting, or modeling. Often the hands know how to solve a riddle with which the intellect has wrestled in vain. (Jung, 1966, para. 180)

As the unconscious mind expresses itself through symbols and imagery, it is through creative art forms that one is able to give form and shape to that which one cannot express in words.

In the 1940s, Margaret Naumburg was the first psychotherapist to establish an art therapy program in the United States to diagnose and treat patients with mental health conditions. She also believed that the most fundamental feelings and thoughts arose from the unconscious and that expressing them through art rather than words could help patients with post-traumatic stress disorder, anxiety, and depression to relieve their symptoms. It was important that the patient-artist interpret their work in discovering their feelings. Since that time, expressive art therapy has been used to diagnose and treat patients with physical and/or emotional problems and those suffering from trauma, aiding communication when they are unable to speak, and ultimately allowing individuals to discover hidden paths on their road to healing.

Expressive art encompasses many forms, such as journaling, music, poetry, dance, and sculpting. All these art forms allow for the expression of a person's innermost feelings. While many have utilized expressive art for purposes of self-discovery, it is also beneficial for stress reduction. Studies have shown that engaging in expressive art decreases levels of cortisol, a hormone that is generally high in times of stress, and increases levels of dopamine, a neurotransmitter that produces a feeling of happiness. Engaging in expressive art forms of any type reduces stress by shifting the individual's focus to the task, allowing them to become mindful of and present with the art.

Psychotherapist Megan Devine (2017) discussed the importance of art and the creative process:

> We look to art, and to story, to help us make sense of the world, especially when what's happened makes no sense. We need images to live into, stories to guide us in the new life that is come. We need the creative process to bear witness to our own reality—to reflect our own pain back to us. (p. 151)

Expressive art therapy is a creative process that forges a pathway to self-discovery and emotional well-being.

THE ARTISTS AND THEIR ILLUSTRATIONS

Each of the following original drawings was created by an individual who suffered the loss of a loved one. The relationship of the bereaved included parent, spouse, child, partner, friend, and soul mate. At the time of the drawing, the death of the loved one had occurred as recently as one month to several years earlier and was the result of an illness, sudden death, or accident. Some of the artists suffered multiple losses of family members.

All the artists were attending a grief support group, individual grief counseling, or classes to further their understanding of the grief process at the time of creating their drawings.

The individuals were asked to draw a picture of what grief looked like to them, creating something visual and tangible that could offer an opportunity for comprehension, clarity, and healing. Each artist presented and interpreted their drawing upon completion.

Attached to each artwork is a short summary of the artist's explanation of their drawing, followed by the author's comments.

Waves

*"Waves wash over me, rendering me powerless,
sending me into the darkest depths."*

The metaphor of grief feeling like ocean waves is commonly used by those suffering the loss of a loved one to express the overwhelming sense of sadness, hopelessness, and despair. By analyzing the attributes of this natural phenomenon, it becomes apparent why this metaphor is so applicable to grief.

The ebb and flow of the ocean represents the vacillation between the highs and lows of emotions felt throughout the grief process. The size of the waves is influenced by outside factors such as wind speed, duration of the wind, and proximity to land. Just as the size of the wave is impacted by external factors, one's grief can be impacted by many factors, as was discussed in the introduction to this book.

In the early stages of grief, waves can be like tsunamis as these powerful waves nearly paralyze bereaved loved ones as they experience shock and denial over their loss. In time, waves continue to be powerful, as loved ones are disoriented in the turbulent water and forced downward into the depths, then finally pushed back to the surface. Many times, one can foresee the waves approaching, with looming dates of anniversaries, birthdays, holidays, and other special days ushering in dark storm clouds and the threat of unsettled seas.

However, there are also "sneaker waves" that appear suddenly and without warning. These waves can be treacherous, as they can sweep the person out to sea to be lost. Noted author and a wife who suddenly lost her husband Helen Reichert Lambin (1998) wrote,

Waves

It is the small sneaky things that get you. . . . With
the big things . . . at least you see them coming.
They don't sneak up from behind and yell "Gotcha!"
. . . Lighted windows in other houses when I walk
the dog at twilight. Reminders of home the way
home once was—the two of us and the children,
around the dinner table. Gotcha! . . . Scraps of
paper in your handwriting. Informal reminders to
yourself about house repairs, projects, and other
things to do. Gotcha! (pp. 99–100)

These unexpected waves of grief can be painful
reminders of the past.

Beyond the metaphorical association of ocean
waves, grief has a physiological association with
waves. Noted psychiatrist Eric Lindemann (1944)
observed that grief creates not only psychological
reactions but also common physiological reactions
related to loss:

The picture shown by persons in acute grief is
remarkably uniform. Common to all is the following
syndrome: sensations of somatic distress occurring
in waves lasting from twenty minutes to an hour at
a time, a feeling of tightness in the throat, choking
with shortness of breath, need for sighing, and an
empty feeling in the abdomen, lack of muscular
power, and an intense subjective distress described
as tension or mental pain. (p. 141)

"Waves"—a common sensation many bereaved
describe, affecting them physically, psychologically,

and physiologically, a reminder of the power and extent of grief.

The Staircase

*"There is a staircase from a dark basement
to a door. The basement represents the
depths of grief and sorrow. The steps shorten
as the pain lessens over time. The door
at the top leads to the rest of my life."*

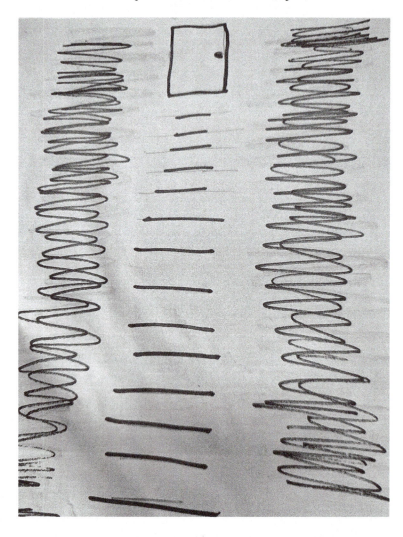

The reference to a basement is meaningful in relationship to the description of grief. The basement is the deepest foundation of a house, giving support to all structures within it. Following the loss of a loved one, grief has the capacity to shake the very foundation of the surviving loved one, threatening their beliefs, identity, security, and perception of the world. Basements are generally thought of as dark and dreary places and often may be frightening. Grief is also associated with darkness, as sadness covers one with a veil, blocking out the sun and joy in life.

The staircase in the drawing is a visual metaphor that invokes a sense of a difficult journey and hardship as one must ascend a steep climb to attain one's destiny. As one looks up from the bottom of the staircase, there is a sense of numerous obstacles ahead. The steps are widely spaced in the drawing, and there is no evidence of a handrail to guide the person and keep them from falling. At times along the grief journey, the person will fall, another reminder that grief is not a linear journey despite the sequential steps toward a new life.

Beyond the closed door is the artist's new life; however, now that door is closed. The closed door represents isolation, loneliness, or an inability to accept the death of the loved one and a readiness to move forward. Although the diminishing size of the stairs represents more resilience along the bereaved's grief journey and decreased pain, opening the door to a "new life" without their loved one can be difficult and frightening. Renowned author and grief specialist David Kessler (2019) wrote,

Allowing yourself only to focus on the past, however miserably, can seem easier, more comfortable than deciding to live fully in a world without your loved one. The negative can be comforting in its familiarity, while deciding to move forward can be frightening because it makes you feel like you're losing your loved one not once, but twice. It's also scary because it requires you to move into the unknown, into a life that is different without that person. (p. 79)

The staircase drawing represents the difficult journey as a person begins the healing process following the loss of a loved one. It is a journey that requires the person's participation, recognition that there will be pitfalls along the way, and a decision to open the door to new possibilities in life.

Grief Is a Nonlinear Journey

"The green line represents my grief journey through darkness and light—a nonlinear journey. The memory of my loved one is ever present throughout. The large 'NO' overlaid on the grief journey signifies the refusal to accept the reality of death."

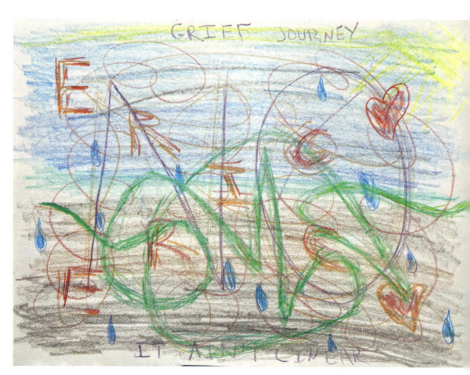

In a time of loss, it is in our nature to make sense of the tragedy that has occurred and to seek to impose some type of structure amid disorder, chaos, and despair. Often, the bereaved look to established models of grieving patterns that will help them understand the grief process. However, these clinical models tend to underestimate the reality of the grief process and do not account for the uniqueness of one's own journey.

One of the most recognized grieving models was set forth by Kübler-Ross, who proposed the five stages of grief: denial, anger, bargaining, depression, and acceptance. Many thought that these stages were to be approached and achieved in a linear fashion, and even her peers had criticized her proposed grief model for this reason. However, Kübler-Ross and Kessler (2007) clarified this model by writing,

> The stages have evolved since their introduction and they have been very misunderstood over the past three decades. They were never meant to help tuck messy emotions into neat packages. They are responses to loss that many people have, but there is not a typical response to loss, as there is no typical loss. Our grief is as individual as our lives. . . . They are tools to help us frame and identify what we may be feeling. But they are not stops on some linear timeline in grief. (p. 7)

The green line in the drawing demonstrates the circuitous, nonlinear route of grief. There may be steps forward in the healing process, only to have triggers send one crashing down into the depths of darkness once again.

At the heart of the grief journey is the deceased loved one. Both tears and hearts surround the loved one, as they represent the love and loss of this beloved person. We grieve the way we love, as one cannot separate one from the other.

The emphatic "NO" in the drawing expresses the refusal to accept the reality of the loved one's death. Acceptance of the loss of a loved one does not come easily or quickly. Acceptance does not mean that one is OK with what has happened; it means that one has come to terms with the loss and recognizes that the loved one is no longer physically present and that the survivor's life is forever changed. The acceptance and recognition not only must be made cognitively but also need to come from the heart:

> The rational mind is not capable of truly under-standing this loss; only the heart has a chance to accept and transform this suffering. For it is not the mind that has been dealt this blow, it is the heart, and it is only there that healing is possible. (Fumia, 2003, p. 131)

Heavy Weight

"Grief felt like a massive weight on me, every minute of the day. It was everything I could do just to walk up straight sometimes."

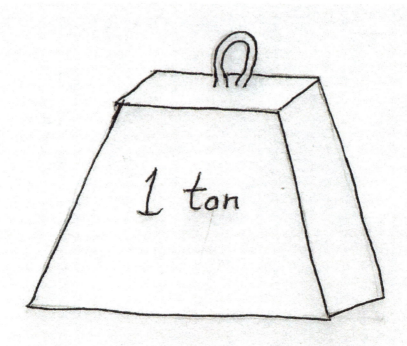

How appropriate that the root for *grief* comes from the Latin word *gravis,* meaning "heavy" or "burdensome."

The death of a loved one will not only have an emotional impact on the person; it will also cause physiological, psychological, and physical distress due to the intricate connection between mind and body. The traumatic event increases activity in the area of the brain called the amygdala, which controls one's emotions, memory, sleep, behavior, mood, and fight-or-flight response. Being in a constant state of fight-or-flight or being hypervigilant can overtax the nervous system and produce feelings of exhaustion. Likewise, the hypothalamus stimulates the adrenal glands, which regulate one's strength and response to stress by way of releasing hormones such as cortisol, adrenaline, and norepinephrine. However, after extended times of stress, the adrenal glands can become depleted, causing adrenal fatigue and low levels of hormones and neurotransmitters, which result in overall feelings of tiredness and exhaustion, making it difficult even to get out of bed and through the day.

Sleep plays an important part in feeling a lack of energy and a heaviness. Poor sleep patterns can be the result of months or years of being a caregiver for a loved one during their illness, not allowing one the luxury of uninterrupted, peaceful sleep. Stress can prevent healthy, restorative sleep, further compromising hormone levels and affecting one's ability to cope and meet the physical and emotional demands of grief.

Feelings of anxiety or depression can give one little incentive to garner enough energy to meet the day. Anhedonia, the state of finding no pleasure in anything in life, can weigh one down and keep one from engaging in life. Bereaved author Molly Fumia (2003) described the debilitating effects of grief:

> I am so tired. These callous circumstances have stolen away my energy and my motivation. I am left without the power to continue moving. I can hardly imagine the strength even to stand in place. I want only to give in to my exhaustion, to sleep and sleep until I can wake up to another, less evil reality. (p. 6)

It is particularly difficult for the newly bereaved to carry this heavy burden when there are so many decisions to be made, so much paperwork to complete, and final arrangements to attend to. These additional demands and stressors only exacerbate the compromised mental and physical well-being of the surviving loved one.

Isolation

"I feel like an incomplete, colorless person, having lost my better half. I am sitting alone in a stark, empty room. The sun is shining outside. Life continues to go on, but I am not able or willing to take part in it."

There is a special union or bond between two people who are married or in partnership, and when that bond is broken due to the death of one of the individuals, the survivor frequently feels that half of them is missing. Whereas they once functioned, lived, and loved as a "we," the survivor is now a "me." Psychotherapist Pamela Ashurst and psychiatrist Zaïda Hall (1989) wrote,

> She is astonished to find herself one person again, instead of being one half of a couple; and yet she is not a whole person, only a lacerated part-person. . . . With the outside world she sees herself as a mere shadow, looking on. Unless she has children, there is no-one in the world for whom she matters most and who matters most to her. (p. 182)

The loss of a loved one involves more than the person; it also involves secondary losses related to the relationship. One grieves what is now missing from this bonded relationship, such as companionship, trust, security, support, the roles and responsibilities that the person filled and provided, and, most of all, love. This combined loss creates an immense void in an individual's life, especially one who has had an established bond with another person for decades. It is little surprise that they sense that part of them is missing upon the death of their loved one.

The drawing shows the person and their immediate surroundings in black and white. The color is gone from their life. Grief has the capacity to remove the zest for life, to lack the ability to see anything positive in life, experience any pleasure or happiness, or have hope for brighter days ahead.

The person sits alone in an empty room, isolated from society by a picture window. For the person who grieves the loss of a loved one, time stops as they try to process the tragedy that has occurred in their life, yet they become painfully aware that the world continues to function normally as if nothing important has happened. Just beyond this thin pane of glass, the sun is shining, flowers bloom, and people are enjoying life. Feelings of resentment and disbelief can be felt as to how this could possibly be when the life of the surviving loved one has been completely shattered.

But this thin pane of glass not only represents a physical boundary between society; it is an emotional boundary as the person states that they are not "able or willing" to take part in society. Some reactions to grief, such as sadness and crying, are passive feelings and behaviors related to the loss—one has little control over these reactions. Then there are responses to grief that involve a more conscious process and decision to reengage in life. At some point along the grief journey, one will need to decide whether one is ready to begin the healing process and reengage with society.

Anger

"Anger, fear, uncertainty, pain, disorientation, inability to breathe, and horror. The world was torn out from under me."

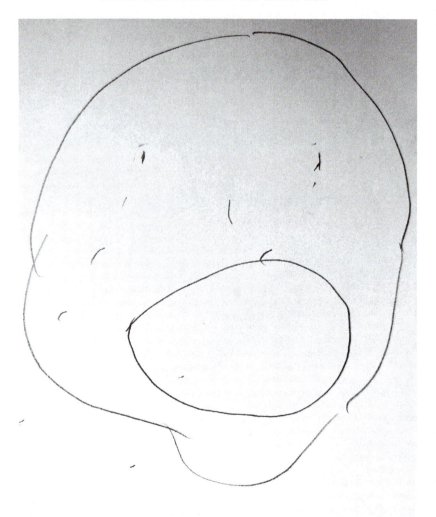

Steven Stosny (1995), a resentment, anger, abuse, and violence counselor, wrote about the anger response to physical and psychological pain:

> Anger is the most powerful of human experience in terms of energy utilization. Anger is the only emotion that activates every organ and muscle group of the body. The biochemicals secreted in the brain in the experience of intense emotion . . . are experienced like an amphetamine and analgesic. The experience of anger numbs pain and provides a surge of energy. (p. 56)

This numbing effect of anger helps one to avoid feelings that may be the very underlying causes of anger: overwhelming sadness over the loss of the loved one, hurt feelings, pain, a sense of helplessness, and fear.

The wide-open mouth on the figure in the drawing depicts the intense feelings that the individual attributes to their grief. "Alarm screams" are defense mechanisms humans and animals share when they are angry, in pain, or afraid. Screaming allows for the release of emotions during events that are extremely stressful: "Grief is visceral, not reasonable: the howling at the center of grief is raw and real. It is love in its most wild form" (Devine, 2017, p. 10).

Anger is a normal response to grief. One may be angry with one's deceased loved one for not taking better care of themselves; angry at the health care system for not diagnosing them earlier and preventing their death; angry at those who were unable to be there to support them through this difficult time;

for some, angry at God for allowing their loved one to suffer and die.

A sense of fear is a natural response as a person faces the unknown having lost a loved one and now living in an unfamiliar world—fear of being alone and having to build a new life, a new identity, and a new meaning and purpose without their loved one.

Although some may feel uncomfortable expressing their anger, it is a necessary component of the healing process of grief:

> Anger is a response to a sense of injustice. Of course, you're angry; whatever has happened to you is unjust. . . . Anger, allowed expression, is simply energy. . . . Shown respect and given room, anger tells a story of love and connection and longing for what is lost. (Devine, 2017, pp. 82–83)

Anger, an appropriate response in bereavement, as the very origin of the word *bereave* lies in a taking away by violence. Anger is an appropriate response to "a sense of injustice."

Unfulfilled Hopes and Dreams

"The image represents the life we had and were going to have. The outlines in the sky were two places we wanted to travel to. The big house represents the hope of buying a house one day. The reflection from the life we once had is the life I have now."

Grief is not only associated with tangible losses, such as the loss of a person, possession, or property, but also accompanies intangible losses, such as the loss of identity, security, hopes, dreams, and expectations. In the case of hopes and dreams, the realization that these are no longer shared with the loved one, were never attained, and may never be achieved in the future is grievous and creates great emotional distress.

In the drawing, the clouds in the sky portray the distant lands hoped to be visited in the future. These dreams of travel are seen in the sky, beyond the reach of the individual.

The landscape represents life prior to the death of the loved one—strong, sturdy trees, fertile green growth, and peaceful rolling hills. The individual's prior life was a space that provided a solid and secure foundation and an opportunity to grow. An empty outline of a house is drawn in the middle, representing the unfulfilled hopes and dreams of purchasing a home and setting down firm roots.

The reflection in the water below the landscape represents the "new life" of the bereaved loved one. The solid foundation that once provided security is gone and has been replaced by water. The reflection mirrors the landscape above, but the image is blurred and undefined as the person attempts to cope with the tremendous loss of the loved one. This critical line of demarcation is a major time of "reflection." Kübler-Ross and Kessler (2007) discussed this dividing line:

Death is a line, a heartbreaking dividing line between the world we and our loved one lived in and the world where they now are. That line of death on a continuum becomes a Before and After mark. A line between time with them and time without them. (p. 204)

Once this dividing line is created, frequently the bereaved is forced to reevaluate their worldview, a set of assumptions that are held to help one make sense of the world and provide the foundation for one's identity, structure, and purpose in life. The set of assumptions provides a person with a sense of the world, of the person's role in it, and of security and control. However, when tragic events occur, these assumptions may be shattered, causing the person to reevaluate the world in which they now live.

Grieving that which is seen and unseen is import-ant, as both will contribute to the overall sense of loss.

Oppressive Outside Forces

"I feel the weight of grief in our home. For years, I worked here to try to save my son's life, and in the end I failed. I did everything I could, but in the end, it leaves me feeling sad and defeated. A remembrance tree is unaffected by the grief in hopes that my son is in a better place."

The death of a child secondary to an accidental drug-related overdose can complicate the grieving process for the surviving parents. Studies have shown that parents suffering such a loss encounter similar stigmatization and isolation treatment to what suicide survivors experience. These "stigmatized" deaths result in grief that is disenfranchised, depriving family members of the ability to share their grief and receive much-needed support from family, friends, and community. Researchers Christine Valentine, Linda Bauld, and Tony Walter (2016) wrote about years of anticipatory grief of family members who were aware of drug use prior to the death of their loved one and how this knowledge caused feelings of despair, a lack of power and control, and hopelessness.

A large, dark, and chaotic mass hovers over a yellow house. Lightning strikes are seen throughout this mass, representing powerful forces, preventing the artist from protecting her son and her home as they strike against the roof of the house. The accidental drug-related death imposes an even greater emotional burden on the surviving loved ones, which is seen and sensed by the artist as a weight upon their home—sadness, defeat, blame, and guilt.

Blame is commonly expressed, especially following cases of accidental death. For some of the bereaved, blaming others for the death of a loved one eliminates their need to show empathy and support for their loss. Blame may be justified in cases of malpractice by health care systems, drunk drivers, or undisputed cases in which the death could have been avoided.

However, oftentimes, blame is used to shift attention away from the person to escape the need to reconcile oneself with the horror of the loss and emotionally connect with others.

Guilt is also a common component of grief. Guilt is based on one's own self-perception and expectations. There may be a sense of guilt or failure in a parent upon the death of a child, as they did not fulfill their duties and responsibilities to protect the child. As with all deaths, many "should've" and "could've" thoughts continuously cycle through the mind, creating doubt as to whether there was a possibility of preventing the death of the loved one.

Kessler (2019) wrote about the tragic loss of his son from an accidental drug overdose and the continued connection that a parent has with their child:

> My son pops up in my mind a lot and I watch the memories of him almost as I would a movie. I replay them and cherish them. Despite my tragic loss, I'm still looking for hope, glimpses of meaning, and for the daylight that might come tomorrow. (p. 158)

Despite the chaos and darkness that loom over the artist's home, the remembrance tree that was planted for her son is spared. The tree is adorned with bright lights, and they illuminate the tree each night, bringing hope and light into the artist's life.

Sadness

"I feel sad and lost and just cannot describe how alone I feel."

The use of stick figures was seen as far back as prehistoric times. It was in the 1920s when an Austrian sociologist, Otto Neurath, developed the idea that an art form with a particular unifying character could transcend languages, words, and phrases that may often be misunderstood. He termed this art form a "universal language." Pictographs or stick figures were widely brought into use by 1972 in the United States. Although these pictures or drawings are simplistic, they are capable of portraying emotions, thoughts, and relationships and are often used in art therapy.

In this drawing, tears and a deep frown elicit feelings of sadness. The character is drawn alone on the page, not only with no other people but with nothing at all.

This artist suffered the loss of both parents. The death of one's parents can pose a unique loss in a person's life. Psychologist Alexander Levy (1999) stated, "Parents provide a unique spot in this planet, which is called 'home' where we can return, if we need to, to be loved, and to feel that we belong" (p. 31). Not only did the person lose their mother and father but they lost also their physical and emotional sense of "home," the one place that they felt safe, secure, and loved. There can also be a loss of family traditions and cultural rituals, many often driven and conducted by the parents. With the loss of their parents, children may become closer, or the bond between them may fracture as they find that the only bond holding them together as a family were the parents, and now that is gone.

Researcher Helen Marshall (2004) noted a unique grieving pattern for those who have lost both parents:

> A phenomenon of a two-staged life transition period was unexpectedly observed which suggests adult children may grieve for their first parent's death in a filtered way through their concern for the grief of the remaining parent; and then, on the death of the second parent, grieve wholly for both parents. (p. 351)

As a wife becomes a widow, a husband a widower, a child of any age, losing both parents, becomes an orphan. There is a connotation of loss and isolation to these new identities. For the child, they are no longer a cherished daughter or son and may feel alone, as this artist, as they have lost the sense of feeling in a place where they "belong."

Broken

"My loved one depended on her walking stick for physical support and on me for moral and emotional support the last years of her life. Upon her death, there was no longer use for the walking stick and I realized that a large part of my purpose in life was caring and supporting her as a 'virtual walking stick' and now feel as broken as the stick."

The death of a loved one results in redefining roles and responsibilities of the surviving loved one. Not only will some individuals need to assume the roles and responsibilities of their deceased loved ones but they will no longer be performing vital roles that they performed prior to their loss. Caregiving for a loved one can be all-consuming, both physically and emotionally—a role that carries a great deal of responsibility and can persist for months or even many years. This major role can become the primary meaning and purpose in life for one who supports their loved one through the end of their life, but the death of the loved one leaves them lost and without a sense of purpose.

Not only are the survivor's meaning and purpose in life lost but their identity is also altered as a husband becomes a widower and a wife a widow. Whatever the relationship, the drastic shift from "us" to "I" is the defining mark when past common hopes, dreams, and goals end and building a "new life"—discovering what is now important in life, what matters, the new hopes and dreams and purpose—begins.

The concept of the "meaning" of life relates to the process of a person attempting to make sense of life and their role in it. The "purpose" in life relates to hopes and dreams that motivate a person to act.

Finding meaning in life was found to be an important aspect of the grieving process. Kessler (2019) wrote *Finding Meaning: The Sixth Stage of Grief* to demonstrate that the grieving process does not end at "acceptance" but continues in finding meaning for the life of the survivor as well as for the death of the loved one.

According to Kessler (2019), "broken crayons can still color, and while our lives may feel broken, we still have the potential to create something beautiful" (p. 96). In Japan, there is an ancient art form called *kintsugi,* meaning "repair with gold." When a valued item would break, pieces would be held together with gold to create something stronger and more beautiful than it was before. This process has been used as a metaphor for healing, as although lives may have been broken and shattered with the loss of loved ones, something more unique and beautiful can be made while continuing to embrace and cherish the memory of the loved one. Finding meaning and purpose in life can provide the "gold" in moving forward in one's new life.

Barriers Moving Forward

"I am stuck between two places: one place of sadness, guilt, fear, and a broken heart, and the other place where I see better days filled with sun, self-care, and laughter. I am trying to merge these two places but remain stuck in the middle."

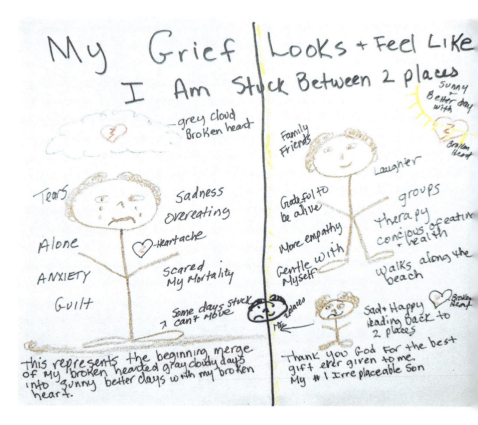

The artist draws herself in two different "places" of grief, surrounded by negative and positive emotions associated with each place. These two places are separated by solid lines: a black line representing the place of sadness, tears, a broken heart, fear, and guilt and a yellow line representing the place of happiness, gratitude, family, and laughter. The artist's face is drawn between these two solid lines, trapped. Although the artist comments that she is trying to "merge these two places," each of these two places is demarcated with solid lines in this drawing, suggesting barriers preventing her from accomplishing this.

The tragic loss of the artist's son may be responsible for difficulty finding hope for the future. The artist mentions that there are some days that she feels "stuck" and cannot move, suggesting that negative memories keep her anchored in the past.

The artist comments on "overeating" in her drawing. "Emotional eating" is a coping mechanism that helps one satisfy emotional needs but not physical hunger. Generally, high-calorie, fatty, and sweet foods trigger the neurotransmitters, such as dopamine, that make one feel good, which prompts one to continue eating. However, studies have shown that emotional eating is based on coping with emotions, avoidance/ distraction, and escape from negative thoughts (Spoor et al., 2007). Although emotional eating may temporarily help one cope emotionally, the guilt, regret, and loss of self-esteem can send the individual into a negative cycle, perpetuating the need for emotional eating.

The drawing of the artist showing her "sad and happy heading back to 2 places" suggests that the artist is not able to feel happiness without her "irreplaceable son." For many individuals, when they first find that they are smiling or utter a laugh during the early stages of their grief, they are shocked and even experience a sense of guilt that they feel any element of joy or happiness in their life after such a devastating loss. They feel that to grieve, one must express sadness to properly honor the loved one and that any expression of happiness is a betrayal of the deceased. However, joy and sadness coexist in grief, and the periods of joy in no way devalue the loss the bereaved has suffered. Both joy and sadness are expressions of love and ways to honor a loved one:

> Your joy is your sorrow unmasked. And the self-same well which your laughter rises was oftentimes filled with your tears. And how else can it be? The deeper that sorrow carves into your being, the more joy you can contain. (Gibran, 2019, p. 6)

Grief as a Black Hole

"I experience grief as a void, akin to a black hole. One tinged with pain seen as a tear and a vacuum, with empty eyes."

The possibility of a massive existence in the universe from which light could not escape was first described by a philosopher by the name of John Mitchell in 1784. In 1967, physicist John Wheeler first coined this phenomenon as a "black hole."

As a metaphor for grief, the defining qualities of the black hole can demonstrate the similarities between the two. A black hole is a celestial region of empty space with a gravitational force so powerful that no matter or light can escape from it. At the perimeter of this black hole is the "event horizon," where time comes to a standstill (Kerr spacetime). Black holes have also been defined as possible doorways into other realities, as types of wormholes.

The drawing illustrates the powerful external forces being exerted on the individual. However, instead of the quantum pressure and gravitational pull present in a black hole, stress and an extreme sense of graveness are felt with grief. As neither matter nor light can escape the gravitational pull of the black hole, one cannot escape grief. Renowned Stanford psychiatrist Irvin D. Yalom (2008) stated, "The pain is there; when we close one door on it, it knocks to come in somewhere else" (pp. 54–55).

Emptiness and an absence of light are shared by the black hole and grief. The emptiness comes from the loss of a loved one and the many secondary losses that accompany it. The world is seen through a veil of darkness with feelings of sadness and hopelessness.

As one nears the event horizon in a black hole, matter fades to invisibility, just as one may lose their identity and question their role in life following the death of a loved one, represented by the empty eyes in the drawing. As time stands still in the black hole, time also feels as though it has stopped for the bereaved, yet the world continues to spin for everyone else.

The theory that black holes may be doorways into alternate realities certainly pertains to the new life that one must begin to build following the loss of a loved one. This "alternate reality" can be disorienting, frightening, and otherworldly at first, one that is difficult to accept.

A black hole, a hole in one's world, a hole created by the immense loss of a loved one, creates an emptiness and void in a new reality. Wrote American poet Edna St. Vincent Millay (1952), "Where you used to be, there is a hole in the world, which I find myself constantly walking around in the daytime, and falling in at night. I miss you like hell" (p. 102).

Relentless

"I feel lost at sea. The waves just keep thrashing my body, and I have no control. Dark clouds are above me, so even when I do or can come up for a quick breath, lightning strikes above me and forces me back under the deep, cold water."

The sudden, unexpected death of a loved one can cause intense feelings of shock, fear, numbness, anxiety, and loss of control. The ability to cope with and process such a loss is greatly diminished as the survivor is overwhelmed with the suddenness of the event, an inability to make sense of what occurred, the unfinished business of life, and no possibility of saying goodbye to their loved one.

In the drawing, the artist expresses these overwhelming feelings—the constant "thrashing" of the turbulent waves against the artist's body and the lack of control to overcome the power of immense grief. The thick, dark clouds obliterate any evidence of blue sky above or escape from the darkness. Painful memories and the discovery of so many secondary losses are shocking reminders of the extent and depth of the loss, perhaps represented by the lightning bolts in the drawing, sending the artist back into the depths of the "cold" water. Instead of the once warm and loving life the artist had, they are now sent down to a scary, cold, empty, and quiet place.

However, this sense of "cold" can also come from friends or family who place blame on the deceased loved one for causing the accident. Instead of giving support, these hurtful comments can result in the bereaved withdrawing to grieve alone. Bereaved mother and founder of the MISS Foundation Joanne Cacciatore (2017) wrote,

> "Man dies of cold, not of darkness." . . . Much more
> dangerous in my already fragile state was the cold-
> ness of others . . . , the dismissive comments, and

the way so many people around me turned away from the ugly, terrifying face of grief. These are the things that unhinged me. Darkness does not kill—but cold can. (pp. 24–25)

Individuals inherently believe that the world is a safe place, and upon hearing the news that a friend or family member had a sudden, accidental death, the first response is to make sense of it by assigning blame to the victim. This "self-protective" mechanism restores the sense of security that nothing bad will happen to them, as the loved one's death was their own fault and not a result of the world being unsafe and unjust. Although these thoughts can be helpful for grieving individuals, their comments can have damaging effects on the surviving loved one, isolating them at the time when they most need support and leaving them in the cold.

A sudden, unexpected death is one of the most difficult to comprehend, as there is no "forewarning ... preparation, no goodbyes, just the loudest absence one could ever imagine" (Kübler-Ross & Kessler, 2007, p. 195).

Fumia (2003) wrote about the shock and relentless horror of loss:

Getting through the day is like walking through a mine field of deadly moments of recollection. Just when I have slipped beneath the surface of remembering, drawn there by the benevolent distractions of daily life, the grim new reality suddenly explodes around me, reminding me that everything is terribly, permanently different. And I must absorb the same first brutal shock, the descending horror over and over again. I am deceived by those instances of forgetfulness, yet I am obviously not ready to live every moment with the inalterable truth. (p. 43)

Loss of Identity

"My feeling of loss toward my partner is tangible. What wasn't so clear has been the secondary loss of my identity—relational, professional, and financial."

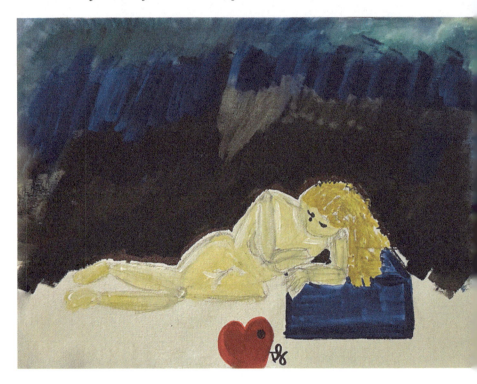

Roles in life are created and assumed in relationship to others; they define the individual and shape their identity. Identity is who the person is in relation to loved ones, community, and the world. With the death of a loved one, those parts of the person defined by the relationship to the deceased are lost, which alters how the person views themselves and how others see them. Clinical psychologist Therese A. Rando (1989) addressed the changes in identity following the loss of a loved one:

> Your identity changes as you slowly make the change from a "we" to an "I." This is caused by the necessity of responding to the new world without the deceased, which demands that you take on new ways of being, thinking, and feeling in the world to reflect the reality that he is dead. You will have to give up or modify certain hopes, expectations, and experiences you had with your loved one, and you must develop new ones. . . . You must adopt new roles, skills, behaviors, and relationships. (p. 239)

In this drawing, the person is unclothed, stripped of her identity. Where once before she was a loving partner, attentive caregiver, and adviser, these roles and responsibilities no longer exist upon the death of the loved one, leaving her feeling vulnerable and exposed to the world.

The oppressive weight of the loss is seen throughout the drawing, expressed by the tear in the person's eye, the hole in her heart, and the thick, dark blanket that drapes over her. The artist references that the female form is being propped up on a pillow made in the lost loved one's favorite color. Although grief is exhausting, as demonstrated by the supine position of the figure in the drawing, she is seeking comfort and support from her relationship to and love of her loved one.

Colors at the top of the drawing become lighter, as they represent to the artist signs of healing and understanding how to recapture and reinvent her identity and find ways to honor the gifts and talents she was given as she makes her way toward brighter days.

Emily Dickinson (1861/1983) wrote the poem "'Hope' Is the Thing with Feathers." This poem employs a metaphor of a bird to symbolize hope. Although life may sometimes be harsh, and individuals can face enduring, tough emotional times, hope is always present. Feathers may seem light, as the colors above the darkness in the drawing, but are ever present, and ever possible, despite the tragedy that one must bear.

The Many Elements of Grief

*"Waves of sadness happen at any time.
Sometimes I feel empty and alone. I have always
been a clear thinker but now feel befuddled. I
have a seesaw of emotions—ups and downs.
I feel as though I am walking in darkness,
trying to access light from this darkness."*

This artist chose a composite drawing of elements of grief. Dr. Alan D. Wolfelt (2021), director of the Center for Loss and Life Transition, wrote that grief is a "deceptively small, simple word for such a wide-ranging, challenging assortment of feelings" (p. 91). Grief affected this recently bereaved artist on multiple levels:

Emotionally. Sadness is the prevalent theme in the drawing, with one figure seen trying to navigate turbulent water and the other about to be overcome by an unexpected, enormous wave. Tears are seen flowing from an eye. The seesaw represents the ever-changing mood swings as one attempts to cope with the shock and reality of a loved one's loss.

Cognitively. The artist comments on being "befuddled" or confused. Noted neuroscientist and psychologist Mary-Frances O'Connor (2022) discussed the neuroscience behind the phenomenon of "grief brain" that accounts for the inability to concentrate and focus. Following the loss of a loved one, a release of stress hormones and neurochemicals prompts a fight-or-flight response. This physiologic response affects the prefrontal cortex of the brain, which is responsible for decision-making, as all focus is now placed on survival. With the brain already overburdened by sadness, pain, and memories secondary to the loss, the bereaved finds it difficult to focus, to read and retain information, and to think clearly.

Socially. The artist draws an empty vessel. The loss of a lifelong partner can feel like losing half of oneself, creating a major void in one's life. The secondary losses of companionship and hopes and dreams for the future attribute to a sense of immense loss.

The artist writes about being in the darkness and seeking light. It is difficult, or nearly impossible, for one to imagine happiness or light in one's future after having suffered a recent loss:

> Slowly, moments in touch with joy accrue by seconds and minutes and later, hours, or even days of contentment. Gradually, we regain the capacity to feel joyful, and we feel this in the same space as grieving. . . . When we do this, we come to see, in this moment or the next, our emotions always moving. The word *emotion* has its roots in the Latin *movere* and *emovere,* meaning "to move through" and "to move out." . . . And when we allow them to move freely, they change, perhaps scarcely, and perhaps gradually—but inevitably. This is grief's most piercing message: *there is no way around—the only way is through.* (Cacciatore, 2017, pp. 52, 54)

The Early Origins of Grief

"I found myself drawing a picture of a little girl, not smiling, with hair sticking out on top of my head, representing my braids. My eyes are wide open, hoping that my parent would see me, but always overlooked, ignored, unloved, and unvalued."

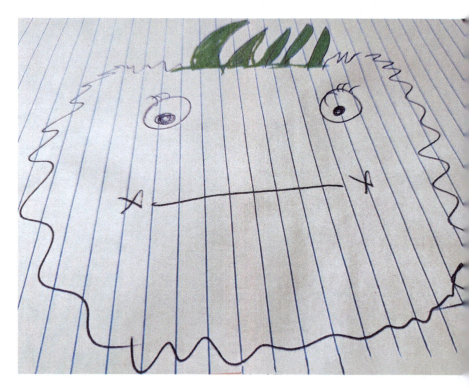

> Our culture may be encouraging you to
> move on, but one of the paradoxes of grief
> is that you have to go backward before you
> can go forward. (Wolfelt, 2021, p. 100)

It was necessary for this artist to look backward to understand the immense sense of loss following the death of her parent. Following the loss of a parent, many recall the special moments they spent with them over the course of their lifetime; the love, support, and encouragement they received from the parent; and the nurturing home the parent provided. However, for some, as for this individual, no such memories come to mind as they grieve.

Developmental needs must be met to ensure that a child attains a sense of belonging, self-worth, and self. *Mirroring* is a process by which the parent imitates the infant's expression and associates it with an emotion, providing validation and approval to the infant. Infants also mirror or mimic those individuals around them to seek a sense of belonging, connection, and empathy. For mirroring to occur, engaged parents or caregivers must reflect and promote the child's developmental growth.

In 1975, Edward Tronick, a developmental psychologist, conducted the Still Face Experiment, which demonstrated the emotional and physical consequences of withholding engagement between an infant and their caregiver. The experiment consisted of having a mother keep a blank face, not responding to her infant despite multiple attempts by the infant to engage her. Ultimately, the infant displays physical distress and then withdraws, turning away with a facial expression of hopelessness.

The artist is grieving the loss of her parent but discovers that she is mourning the loss of the relationship she did not have with that parent as a child and young adult. She drew grief represented as a small girl with no smile, eyes seeking acknowledgment but never receiving engagement, resulting in a poorly defined sense of self represented by the squiggly outlines of her face. Children depend on their caregivers for the development of their self-worth, self- esteem, and validation.

Difficult relationships can create difficult emotions upon the death of a loved one. Processing and acknowledging the person and what might have been in the past is important in mourning the significant losses that have occurred in one's life.

Loss of Hope

"I felt that all hope was lost following the death of my loved one: the hope for a cure, the hope for realizing all our plans and dreams for the future, and for our happily ever after."

"What ever happened to happily ever after?
As it turns out, that was the cruelest part
of the fairy tale. (Fumia, 2003, p. 33)

Hope is one of the fundamental parts of being human. It provides motivation to seek and create a better future and to look beyond the immediate present. Hope brings meaning and shapes a person's life by defining life goals and aspirations. Not only does this positive expectation of future improvement in one's life drive one to seek ways to achieve one's goals but the sense of "hope" has been found to benefit one's current state of mind.

However, according to Wolfelt (2021), just as "love and grief are two sides of the same precious coin" (pp. 97–98), hope and despair are also directly linked. "Hope is not possible without the temptation to feel despair. . . . They are two poles of perpetual oscillation" (Szabat & Knox, 2021, p. 537).

There is a continuum between despair and hope. Despair reflects on the past to determine the future, whereas hope looks to the future to imagine all the possibilities. As one grieves the loss of a loved one, one reflects on the past and everything one has lost: a life shared, traditions, and myriad secondary losses. The memories of the past and the bleak present prevent one from seeing any hope for the future without the loved one.

For those who have lost loved ones with a terminal illness, the loss of hope may occur upon the transition to hospice care, when there is no longer a focus on a cure, intervention, or treatment for their loved one.

The bereaved may feel hopelessness or despair, as there are no further options or hope for the loved one. The sudden death of a loved one claims all future hopes, dreams, and goals not only for that loved one but also for the bereaved.

Although the newly bereaved experience little or no hope following the loss of a loved one, as they begin to search for meaning in their new lives without their loved ones, new goals begin to appear, giving rise to a glimmer of hope. English poet and novelist Martin Tupper (1867) wrote, "Though the breath of disappointment should chill the sanguine heart, speedily it glows by the warm embers of hope" (p. 13).

Intertwining of Love and Grief

"My ring is a double knot, resembling the connection between love and grief. The wavy rope side of the knot is my grief. The smooth side of the knot represents the love for my daughter."

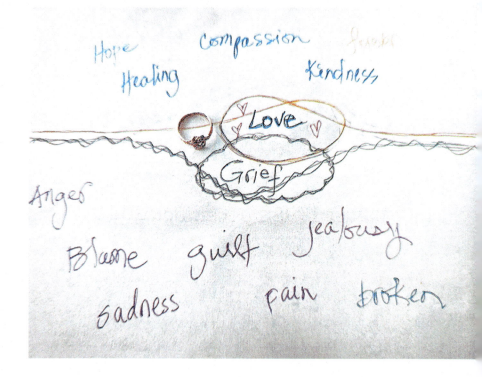

The love knot ring symbolizes an unbreakable bond between two loves. This everlasting relationship has no beginning and no end. This ring shares many attributes of grief, as there is no end to grief—the survivor will always continue to sense the loss of this beloved person. Yet, the bereaved will learn how to develop a continuing bond with their loved one and bring them forward into their new life.

The artist draws two ropes of the ring. One rope, designated "love," represents the young daughter she tragically lost. This rope is drawn in smooth, gold pencil, surrounded by hearts and positive affirmations of hope, healing, and kindness. One outstanding word written in gold is "forever." It appears to be significant that this "rope," which signifies her daughter, is highlighted in gold along with the word "forever," as this color connotes how precious and valued she is to the artist.

The second rope is frayed, labeled "grief," representing the artist. This rope is surrounded by negative feelings and emotions of guilt, blame, anger, sadness, jealousy, and pain. One word is written in black—"broken," expressing the immense loss of her young daughter.

Feelings of guilt and blame are frequently seen in cases when the loved one's death occurred under tragic circumstances:

> Trauma can shatter previously positive beliefs about the self, world, and others (or reinforce previously negative ones). This is a truly terrifying experience leaving a survivor struggling with unfamiliar (or

all too familiar) notions of uncertainty, unpredict-ability, and uncontrollable injustice in the world. Understandably, the trauma survivor may look for a meaning that makes the world feel more control-lable, predictable, and just so that their previous view of their world is not breached. For example, they might believe that the negative outcome would not have occurred if they had just acted differently, giving rise to self-blame and guilt. (Young et al., 2021, p. 2)

Although these negative feelings that accompany complicated grief related to sudden and traumatic losses have "frayed" the rope in this artist's love knot ring, the unbreakable bond with her daughter remains intact, and their relationship remains intertwined.

Circle of Grief

*"I am at the vortex of the circle of grief. Grief
surrounds me, growing larger as it encompasses
more of my life every day. Feelings of sadness,
infinite mourning, yet a perspective of empowerment
to move forward through the spiral of grief."*

This artist's drawing presents many symbolic elements of grief, most notable being the circle. There is no end to grief. Frequently, many mention "closure" as an end point of grief where mourning can cease and life can begin again. However, professor Nancy Berns (2011) wrote, "Closure talk frames grief as bad and therefore something that needs to end. This rhetoric implies that closure exists and it is possible, good, desirable, and necessary" (p. 51). However, the loss of a loved one will have a lifelong effect on the person, and developing continued bonds with the loved one will help in incorporating them into the bereaved's new life as they move forward. Kübler-Ross and Kessler (2007) wrote,

> The reality is that you will grieve forever. You will not "get over" the loss of a loved one; you will learn to live with it. You will heal, and you will rebuild yourself around the loss you have suffered. You will be whole again, but you will never be the same. Nor should you be the same, nor would you want to. (p. 230)

Not only is there special meaning to what is written within this circle but there is also significance in the location and size of the words, giving symbolic meaning to grief. The artist mentions being at the "vortex" of the circle. This location of the circle is the area of most turbulence and intensity, with decreasing intensity as it dissipates to the outer boundaries. The word "grief" is written in condensed letters, signifying intensity. Spiraling outward, the "grief" letters become larger, instead of smaller as expected. The artist stated that grief did not become larger but occupied a greater portion of day-to-day life. Following the loss of a loved one, the bereaved are forced to deal with settling estates; arranging for funerals, memorials, or celebrations of life; and completing the extensive paperwork associated with a loved one's death. Then there is the discovery of all the secondary losses that accompany the loss, taking on the roles and responsibilities of the loved one, and adjusting to one's "new life." Grief is no longer focused only on the loss of the loved one but affects a much broader area of the survivor's life.

The artist wrote three reflections within the circle:

"Bye Bye Love, Hello Loneliness, I think I'm going to Cry" (lyrics taken from the Everly Brothers song "Bye Bye Love")

"Infinite mourning, every morning, every afternoon, every evening, you are in my mind and heart every second of every day"

"Grieving in circles, my days like a circuit with no off switch, yet powers me to go on as you would want me to as you did every day"

The artist randomly wrote these statements within the circle; however, the statement of loneliness and sadness was written closest to the vortex of the circle, the mention of mourning in the middle, and the statement of moving forward at the outer periphery. These three statements follow the trajectory of grief as one grieves the loss of a loved one, begins to process the enormous loss, and eventually discovers the power and strength to move forward in one's new life.

Worry

"After having the security and safety, in a loving relationship with my husband for over forty years, his death left me feeling insecure, vulnerable, and lost with so many worries."

°No one ever told me that grief felt so
like fear. (Lewis, 1961, p. 3)

Lewis's comment references the physiologic response
that grief has, similar to fear, which is the fight-or-
flight response during instances of perceived threat
or present danger. Although fear and anxiety share
this physiologic response, fear is based in present
circumstances, whereas anxiety is focused on antici-
pating future threats. Worry is the feeling of concern
or uneasiness in relationship to a specific situation
or problem. There can be a fine line between worry
and anxiety, as a person can no longer control their
concern, producing a physiological response that
can interfere with their ability to cope and function.
    Author and grief therapist Claire Bidwell Smith
(2020) discussed the prevalence and importance of
anxiety following the death of a loved one and how
anxiety can impact the healing process:

> It makes sense that loss causes anxiety. Losing
> someone we love is one of the most difficult things
> we will ever experience during our lifetime. The
> impact of this loss permeates all areas of our
> life and can often bring us to a standstill. Death
> reminds us that our lives are nothing if not precar-
> ious and that everything can change at a moment's
> notice. (p. 14)

This artist's drawing highlights many common
thoughts that cause anxiety for many survivors.
Mortality salience—the awareness of our own

mortality—has the capacity to create a great deal of anxiety after experiencing the death of a loved one. The realization that death is inevitable can result in terror, as most individuals spend their lives avoiding contemplating this reality.

The death of a loved one represents not only the loss of the person but also the death of the person the survivor once was and the life they had prior to the death. Nothing will ever be the same. Coming to terms with this drastic change creates a feeling of loss of control and an overall sense of uncertainty and insecurity for one's new life and future.

In the artist's drawing, the person is drawn with her eyes closed, unaware of her current surroundings. Anxiety is future oriented—a time of uncertainty, imaginary threats, and loss of control. Opening one's eyes and being mindful of the present can offer one a sense of control and inner peace. Said Buddha, "The secret of health for both mind and body is not to mourn for the past, worry about the future, or anticipate troubles, but to live in the present most wisely and earnestly."

Hope for Growth and Healing

"An evergreen plant was given to my daughter. It died a few weeks following the death of my daughter. But after one year, new signs of green growth appeared, which gives me hope that one day, I, too, will feel alive once again after feeling dead inside. My mother's tears and my continued care and hope have kept this plant alive."

This artist chose an evergreen plant to represent the grief she experienced following the loss of her daughter. The evergreen is symbolic of life and hope, and the reference to this plant applies not only to the life and death of her daughter but also to the life and death of the artist's self.

The evergreen plant or tree plays a special part in the celebration of the winter holidays. For the daughter, the evergreen tree was a personal favorite and had special meaning for her. The death of this evergreen, which so closely followed the death of the artist's daughter, represented the death of her daughter, her joy in life, and her hopes for her future.

However, not only did the tree represent the daughter's death; the artist also felt "dead inside" upon her daughter's loss. The loss of a child can leave a parent without a sense of identity or meaning and purpose in life. Stephen J. Freeman (2005), professor of counseling at California State University, Sacramento, wrote,

> Parent–child attachment begins at conception and continues a lifetime. Whatever the age, the death of a child is seen as one of the most negative life experiences that an individual can encounter. Grieving is complicated, owing to the fact that the loss is both internal—a loss of hope for the future—and external—the loss of an individual who is an extension of ourselves. (p. 109)

But just as this plant is a symbol of life and hope, other symbols in the drawing represent nurturing, growth, and healing to sustain life and give hope. Mourning is the outward expression of grief. The tears expressed by the artist and the family member offer support and healing during this difficult time. The artist continues to care for the evergreen, representing the continuing bond with her daughter, which is vital to the grief and healing processes.

Mourning is an active process, and participating in this process can result in a transformation of the surviving loved one. Kessler (2019) wrote about transformation, "Although your relationship with your loved one will change after death, it will also continue, no matter what. The challenge will be to make it a meaningful one" (p. 66).

New growth, new life, and new hope for the future following the loss of a loved one involve tending to one's grief, just as one would nurture a living plant.

Broken Heart

*"My heart feels broken having lost my
friend and partner after so many years, yet
I have always felt connected to her."*

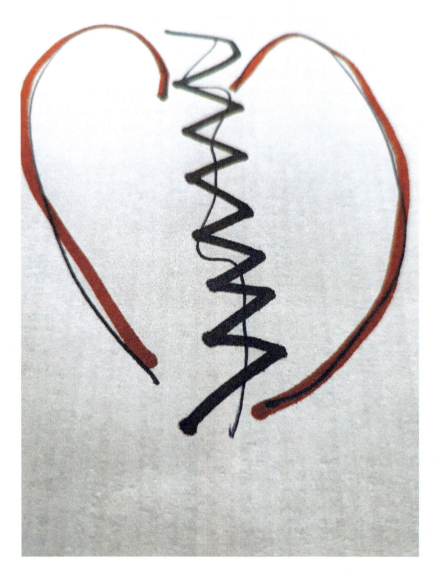

The "broken heart" has been used as a metaphor to depict the crushing emotional and physical pain that accompanies the loss of a loved one. However, heartbreak is more than just a metaphor. Brain imaging studies have shown that the neural circuits responsible for conducting physical and emotional pain share the same pathways in the brain, so when an individual is experiencing a devastating event, such as the loss of a loved one, it is common to sense both physical and emotional pain simultaneously.

Studies have also shown that the conflict between the dual activation of the sympathetic and parasympathetic systems can cause stress on the cardiac system. The surge of stress hormones can trigger cardiac abnormalities, resulting in stress cardiomyopathy, also known as *Takotsubo syndrome,* which can result in decreased cardiac function, arrhythmia, and even death.

Although the artist draws a broken heart, the severed halves of the heart remain intact. The artist comments that a connection with the loved one persisted throughout their relationship and continues even after death. Author Mitch Albom (1997) wrote,

As long as we can love each other, and remember the feeling of love we had, we can die without ever really going away. All the love you created is still there. All the memories are still there. You live on—in the hearts of everyone you have touched and nurtured while you were here. . . . Death ends a life, not a relationship. (p. 174)

Freud's "grief work" proposed the breaking of ties that bind the deceased with the surviving loved one to expedite the grieving process. However, in 1996, professors Dennis Klass, Phyllis Silverman, and Steven Nickman found that it was important in the healing process to continue the relationship with the deceased loved one—not relinquishing it but modifying it as it evolves over time.

Professor of philosophy and former president of the Association for Death Education and Counseling Thomas Attig (2011) discussed the healing benefits of maintaining the bond with a lost loved one:

> We can continue to "have" what we have "lost," that is, a continuing, albeit transformed, love for the deceased. We have not truly lost our years of living with the deceased or our memories. Nor have we lost their influences, the inspirations, the values, and the meanings embodied in the lives. We can actively incorporate these into new patterns of living that include the transformed but abiding relationships with those we have cared about and loved. (p. 189)

A broken heart—held together with memories, the essence, and the love of the departed loved one.

Absence

"I am greeted with deafening silence when I walk through the door, expecting your voice. Your usual side of the bed remains empty, and there is a missing chair at the dining room table. I sense your absence everywhere."

Absence is different than a void. A void is a space that holds nothing, whereas an absence represents a space where something once was. It is the paradox of the presence of absence and the absence of presence, where you see an object, and that object you see is also what is not there. In the drawing, the person recognizes that their loved one is absent from the bed next to them and no longer sitting at the table, therefore also recognizing the absence of presence in the bed and at the table.

An old Portuguese word was coined in the fifteenth century, as many voyagers set sail and never returned. Families were left not knowing what had happened to their loved ones, longing for their return and their presence once again. The poorly defined word for this feeling is *saudade,* or presence of absence.

The recognition of this absence causes the bereaved to fill this space with the longing for their loved one, with feelings of sadness, and reminds them of the immensity of what had happened in their life.

"Her absence is like the sky, spread over every-thing"—C. S. Lewis (1961, p. 11) described how the absence of a loved one touches every part of one's being. Grief is the yearning not only for the person but also for the absence of the comforting touch of their hand, the absence of their voice, as mentioned in the drawing, welcoming them as they arrive "home," letting them know that they are now in a loving, secure, and safe environment. The voice of a loved one also has the capacity to make the partner feel valued, heard, seen, and understood, producing a strong foundation for a loving relationship. The absence of this voice creates difficulties as the bereaved partner is forced to make significant decisions alone without this "second opinion" in their new life. What they may miss most in this absence of voice are the three words they will never hear again from their loved one: "I love you."

Following the death of his wife, author William Bridges described the powerful feelings rendered by her absence:

> Now her absence was palpable. It was a tangible fact that she wasn't there, and that fact made her emotional presence very powerful. It was less that I had feelings or thoughts about her than that I perceived her in absentia. It was as though there was always nearby, a shape cut out of space, an empty silhouette of nothingness shaped exactly like her. (quoted in Panagotacos, 2014, p. 8)

THE ESSENCE OF GRIEF

These drawings offer only a glimpse into the immense effect grief has on the lives of those who have suffered the loss of a loved one and testify to the fact that the concept of grief cannot be contained within a defined set of parameters.

Metaphorically speaking, grief was compared to a "black hole" and the deepest depths of the ocean: each, mysteriously dark, not fully understood or explored. How fitting to use these two extremes to describe grief, as grief is cloaked in darkness and is enigmatic.

The continuum of time relates to grief. Past, present, and future hold challenges for those who grieve. Difficult past relationships create complications for those who now grieve a loved one. The sense of time standing still while the rest of the world moves on as if nothing important has happened leads to resentment. The future can appear frightening and unattainable, keeping a survivor living in the past and unable to move forward in their new life.

A wide range of colors in the drawings highlight other aspects of grief: sadness; oppression; lack of interest in or zest for life; hope, growth, and love.

Grief was shown to create a wide range of emotions and physical abnormalities ranging from the most basic human emotion of anger to fear, anxiety, sadness, pain, fatigue, emotional eating, guilt, and blame.

The numerous secondary losses, such as the loss of identity, finances, relationships, meaning and purpose in life, and future hopes and dreams, demonstrate the overarching impact that grief has on one's life.

Another important aspect of grief that the drawings make apparent is that not only are tangible losses grieved but so also are those things that were never experienced or realized—hopes, dreams, future plans, places never visited, and words never said. What never happened can also be painful and must be grieved. The concept of presence of absence and absence of presence is also an element of grief. What is not there is a painful and often constant reminder of the being who was once there and is no longer.

Each artist perceived the very essence of grief in a distinctly individual manner and supported Kessler's (2019) statement that "each person's grief is as unique as their fingerprints" (p. 29).

FINAL REFLECTION

"What does grief look like to you?" When this artwork assignment was posed to these bereaved individuals, they met it with some hesitation and consternation. Many felt that they did not have the artistic skill to properly express their feelings. For some, an image immediately came to mind, whereas others had difficulty even visualizing what grief felt and looked like to them; however, once they put pencil to paper, those who had difficulty beginning the assignment were amazed at how their hands directed them. This reinforces Jung's analytic theory that the unconscious drives the "hand" that produces something tangible, enabling the artist to gain insight into their emotions.

As the artists presented their drawings and reflected on their meaning, there were many profound moments of discovery and much insight into the stumbling blocks that prevented the artists from moving forward along their grief journeys. These "aha moments" triggered hope and the strength to journey forward.

Hidden within each of these amazing drawings is a vision of self-discovery, for the artwork is looking into the eye of grief, where the true essence of grief can be found, allowing one to find one's way along a path of healing.

ACKNOWLEDGMENTS

My heartfelt gratitude and appreciation go to all the artists who contributed their drawings to this book, for without them, this book would not exist. Thank you for your trust in allowing me to share a part of your story. It has been an honor and a privilege to walk with you along your grief journey. I also wish to express many thanks to my copy editor, Holly Monteith. Her editorial skills, creative design, interest, support, and guidance were instrumental and much appreciated throughout the publishing process.

REFERENCES

Albom, M. (1997). *Tuesdays with Morrie: An old man, a young man, and life's greatest lesson*. Doubleday.

Ashurst, P., & Hall, Z. (1989). *Understanding women in distress*. Routledge.

Attig, T. (2011). *How we grieve: Relearning the world* (Rev. ed.). Oxford University Press.

Berns, N. (2011). Chasing "closure." *Contexts, 10*(4), 48–53. https://doi.org/10.1177/1536504211427869

Cacciatore, J. (2017). *Bearing the unbearable: Love, loss, and the heartbreaking path of grief*. Wisdom.

Devine, M. (2017). *It's OK that you're not OK: Meeting grief and loss in a culture that doesn't understand*. Sounds True.

Dickinson, E. (1983). "Hope" is the thing with feathers. In T. H. Johnson (Ed.), *The complete poems of Emily Dickinson*. Belknap Press of Harvard University Press. (Original work published 1861)

Freeman, S. J. (2005). *Grief and loss: Understanding the journey*. Brooks/Cole.

Fumia, M. (2003). *Safe passage: Words to help the grieving*. Conari Press.

References

Gibran, K. (2019). On joy and sorrow. In *The prophet* (p. 6). Dreamscape Media.

Jung, C. G. (1966). *The collected works of C. G. Jung* (G. Adler, M. Fordham, H. Read, & W. McGuire, Eds.; R. F. C. Hull, Trans.; 2nd ed., Vol. 16). Princeton University Press.

Kessler, D. (2019). *Finding meaning: The sixth stage of grief.* Scribner.

Klass, D., Silverman, P. R., & Nickman, S. L. (Eds.). (1996). *Continuing bonds: New understandings of grief.* Taylor & Francis.

Kübler-Ross, E. (1975). *Death: The final stage of growth.* Simon & Schuster.

Kübler-Ross, E., & Kessler, D. (2007). *On grief and grieving: Finding the meaning of grief through the five stages of loss.* Scribner.

Lambin, H. R. (1998). *The death of a husband: Reflections for a grieving wife.* ACTA.

Levy, A. (1999). *The orphaned adult: Understanding and coping with grief and change after the death of our parents.* Da Capo Press.

Lewis, C. S. (1961). *A grief observed.* Harper One.

Lindemann, E. (1944). Symptomatology and management of acute grief. *American Journal of Psychiatry, 101*(2), 141–148. https://doi.org/10.1176/ajp.101.2.141

Marshall, H. (2004). Midlife loss of parents: The transition from adult child to orphan. *Ageing International, 29*(4), 351–367. https://doi.org/10.1007/s12126-004-1004-5

Millay, E. (1952). *Letters of Edna St. Vincent Millay* (A. R. Macdougall, Ed.). Harper.

References

O'Connor, M.-F. (2022). *The grieving brain: The surprising science of how we learn from love and loss.* HarperCollins.

Panagotacos, V. (2014). *Gaining traction: Starting over after the death of your life partner.* Steady Guide Press.

Rando, T. A. (1989). *How to go on living when someone you love dies.* Bantam Books.

Smith, C. B. (2020). *Anxiety: The missing stage of grief—a revolutionary approach to understanding and healing the impact of loss.* Hachette Books.

Spoor, S. T. P., Bekker, M. H. J., van Strien, T., & van Heck, G. L. (2007). Relations between negative affect, coping, and emotional eating. *Appetite, 48*(3), 368–376. https://doi.org/10.1016/j.appet.2006.10.005

Stosny, S. (1995). *Treating attachment abuse: A compassionate approach.* Springer.

Szabat, M., & Knox, J. L. (2021). Shades of hope: Marcel's notion of hope in end-of-life care. *Medicine, Health Care, and Philosophy, 24,* 529–542. https://doi.org/10.1007/s11019-021-10036-1

Tupper, M. (1867). On anticipation. In *Proverbial philosophy* (p. 13). Edward Moxon.

Valentine, C., Bauld, L., & Walter, T. (2016). Bereavement following substance misuse: A disenfranchised grief. *Omega—Journal of Death and Dying, 72*(4), 283–301. https://doi.org/10.1177/0030222815625174

Wolfelt, A. D. (2021). *Understanding your grief: Ten essential touchstones for finding hope and healing your heart* (2nd ed.). Companion Press.

Yalom, I. D. (2008). *Staring at the sun: Overcoming the terror of death.* Jossey-Bass.

References

Young, K., Chessell, Z. J., Chisholm, A., Grady, F., Akbar, S., Vann, M., Rouf, K., & Dixon, L. (2021). A cognitive behavioural therapy (CBT) approach for working with strong feelings of guilt after traumatic events. *Cognitive Behaviour Therapist, 14*(26), 1–21. https://doi.org/10.1017/S1754470X21000192

Marlene A. Enderlein's professional career began in cardiology. She was fortunate to be involved in pediatric cardiology during its infancy, working with a team of dedicated pediatric cardiologists and surgeons to establish guidelines to assist in diagnosing and managing infants and children with congenital heart disease. She authored and coauthored numerous medical journal articles and chapters in medical textbooks that have become standard references today. She worked with many subspecialties, teaching them skills to diagnose congenital heart disease from in utero to aiding the treatment in the adult with congenital heart disease. She retired in 2017 after thirty-three years.

Following numerous personal losses, Marlene decided to pursue her interest in how loss affects the mind–body–spirit. She attended graduate school and received her master's degree in mental health and wellness with an emphasis in grief and bereavement. She currently is a volunteer bereavement counselor with hospice.

Marlene enjoys gardening, reading, and all that nature has to offer in the San Francisco Bay area.

Made in the USA
Las Vegas, NV
15 March 2024

87201151R10075